ORIGINAL MIND

IMAGINING IKKYU'S WILD
WAYS

Martin Stepek was born in Scotland, at
Cambuslang near Glasgow on 19 February
1959. He started writing while at school but
never sought to publish. Instead he began his
career as a company director in his father's
family business. It was not until 2012 at the
age of 53 that he published his first book, the
epic poem *For There is Hope*, followed by
Mindful Living (2014), *Mindful Poems* ((2015)
and *Mindful Living 2* (2015). He collaborated
online with the Polish-American poet John
Guzlowski, resulting in their joint volume of
micro poems *Waiting for Guzlowski* (2017). His
latest works are *A Pocket Guide to a Mindful Life*
(2018), *Steps to a Mindful Life* (2018), *Towards a
Mindful Society: The Sunday Herald Collection*
(2018), *Steps to a Mindful Life, Vol 2* (2019), and
Original Mind: Imagining Ikkyu's Wild Ways
(2019)

By the same author

POETRY

For There is Hope

Mindful Poems

Waiting for Guzlowski

Original Mind: Imagining Ikkyu's Wild Ways

MINDFULNESS

Mindful Living

Mindful Living 2

A Pocket Guide to a Mindful Life

Steps to a Mindful Life

Towards a Mindful Society: The Sunday Herald Collection

Steps to a Mindful Life, Vol 2

MARTIN STEPEK

Original Mind

Imagining Ikkyu's Wild Ways

CADZOW-HACZOW BOOKS

CADZOW-HACZOW BOOKS

Published in Cadzow-Haczow Books 2019

Printed in Great Britain

1

Ikkyu gets on his bike

And cycles through the forest

This hasn't been invented yet

He thinks to himself

But who cares?

2

Ikkyu on a little moped

Going twenty miles per hour

Singing to himself in full throttle

Born to be wi-i-ld

3

Ikkyu takes a bath

Makes sure his private parts are clean

I'll be using these later tonight

Breaking my vows for pleasure.

4

Naughty Ikkyu caresses the woman

With whom he has just spent

Five hours in bed

Instead of meditating in the temple.

He had another place to worship.

5

Ikkyu looks at the wind and rain.

Nothing concerns me he says

And steps out to get soaked

On a three-hour hike

To his friend the Abbott.

6

Ikkyu is hungry

Mad monk thinks it's OK

Not to take care of himself

7

Ikkyu eats a whole cabbage.

Thanks the Cabbage Gods

Laughs at the idea

Of a Cabbage God

But bows low.

8

Ikkyu watches the birds play

I wish I could be a bird he thinks

I'd fly to the Buddha

In his Jade Heaven

9

Ikkyu goes for a bath

There's no water in the tub

There's no tub

Still he is purified

10

Ikkyu has an ice cream

For the first time

He loves it to bits

Never again he says.

11

Ikkyu has a headache

Atishoo! He sneezes violently

It clears his head

Enlightened! he shouts triumphantly

12

Ikkyu is the elephant in the room

Zen and sex and moaning and peace

The walking maniac monk

13

Ikkyu takes a photograph

Of his illegitimate son.

How do I explain this to the Abbott?

he wonders, not caring a jot.

14

Ikkyu pretends he's not really Ikkyu.

I'm a Scottish poet

From the twenty-first century

And falls to the floor laughing

15

Ikkyu sneaks up on the Polish-American.

Who the hell are you

To write poems about me?

I am Ikkyu

Guzlowski replies

We are all of us Ikkyu.

16

Ikkyu is a banana

All skin and fruit

Yellow on the outside

Mush in the centre.

He doesn't care.

17

Ikkyu goes on a mountain bike

Visits the Abbott down the valley

Tears stream down his cheeks

My mistress has died of cholera

He weeps

But he accepts and transforms it.

18

Ikkyu visits the new Abbott

Do I know you? You look familiar.

The Abbott replies

I am you, old fool.

19

Ikkyu goes to vote

Then remembers

No democracy here.

Slips his voting paper

into the back pocket

Of his Levi jeans.

20

It's Ikkyu's 21st birthday.

Drunk and thoroughly debauched

He'll put it down to experience

From which he'll never learn

21

Dinner's ready Ikkyu

His mistress shouts from the kitchen.

Will be there in a minute

Am just finishing a meditation

He says

Dancing in front of the mirror

To Creedence's *Born on the Bayou*

22

Ikkyu takes a swig of black rum

It's rough as hell

Nirvana!

23

Ikkyu sees it's raining outside.

His spirits sink, he shakes his head.

Buddha never knew days like this

He says.

24

Ikkyu coughs.

He knows he's got a cold.

What if it's cancer?

His mind's trying to wreck his day.

Cancer means death,

Death means nothing

Bring it on.

25

Ikkyu thinks to himself

I'm not really Ikkyu.

It's just a label

Someone applied to me

Like they do at an airport

To your luggage

26

Ikkyu gets stuck at Paddington Station

He has a sign round his neck

Please look after this monk.

Thank You.

Mr. and Mrs Brown see him

And ask him where he is from.

Darkest Japan.

There's a fake Ikkyu running around

Drinking too much

And sleeping with women.

He's dressed in the monk's robes.

Ah, no, it is the real Ikkyu

Pretending to be a fake.

28

Ikkyu buys a beer.

And a drink for everyone in the bar

He shouts.

Everyone gets their drink

And hail the monk's magnanimity.

You're welcome he says

I have no money.

29

Ikkyu sleeps under a canopy of trees

Head on a rock

The deer walk softly past him,

Know he is precious

They don't want to disturb him.

30

Ikkyu dreams of skeletons

Living ones

The undead

Waking up, he knows

That's me in this moment.

The undead in a dream.

31

Ikkyu sees a penguin

What the fuck is that?

I shouldn't swear

He knows it's not Right Speech

But really, what the fuck is that?

32

Ikkyu finishes off copulating

With the schoolteacher down the road.

He meditates on lust

Knows it's so wrong

But my, how she can teach a lesson.

33

There's a picnic by the lake.

Ikkyu is nowhere to be seen.

He has pledged himself to poverty

And seeks refuge in a cave.

He'll beg for their scraps this evening.

34

Ikkyu is dead still

One tiny pause between life

and death

One tiny pause between death

And infinite life.

35

In the middle of a pond

Ikkyu sits like a giant frog

Ribbit

he says

And the lily pads become enlightened

36

Ikkyu drinks up every last drop

Of water from a dirty pond.

He is sick for the next four days.

Ribbit

he says

It's a frog's life.

37

Ikkyu cuts the grass

with his new lawnmower.

It's the latest 15th century model

And in Japan they are ahead of the times.

Moo, its engines roar.

38

Ikkyu considers his name.

Ikk yu he thinks

Why not Yu Ikk?

Rhymes with Buick

Which won't come into existence

For several centuries yet

But Ikkyu doesn't mind.

He's a world-renowned brand

A cool vehicle

In his own way

39

Ikkyu sneezes violently again.

Criticises himself for doing such a thing

Atishoo, he reflects.

Sounds a bit like Ikkyu.

How poetic the world would be

If all people sneezed my name

40

Ikkyu is 623 years old today,

Doesn't look a day over fifty.

He puts it down to sex, green tea and rock n roll.

41

In the Whirlies Roundabout

In East Kilbride

Ikkyu leads a meditation

on the emptiness of all things.

The roundabout disappears

And all hell lets loose on the road.

It's rush hour.

42

Ikkyu likes rhubarb.

Rhubarb, he was fond of saying

Is like the Buddha

Very good for you

But better with some sugar on top.

43

Ikkyu likes his beer too much.

No such thing as too much

He says as he throws up

On the temple settee.

44

Drink for drink's sake

Murmured Ikkyu

Keeling over the offering bowl for the third time.

Art for art's sake

And drink for drink's sake

45

Ikkyu voted for Scottish Independence

On a flying time-travel visit to 2014.

Maybe next time he says

But it doesn't matter.

We all die in the end

And the end is Nigh

Whenever Nigh is.

Anyway I've been to Scotland and it's not bad

But not as good as the outdoor swimming pool in Girona.

46

Ikkyu hasn't shaved for days.

Nor cut his hair.

He's going through a hippy phase

Having listened to David Crosby's song

About this moral dilemma.

47

The Big Bad Wolf is on the prowl.

Reports of him blowing down the straw house.

Even the wooden house wasn't strong enough

To withstand his power.

Ikkyu settles him down

Asks him to consider the karma of his selfish and destructive intentions.

Wow, blow me down says the wolf.

48

A pause is simply an activity which isn't recorded

Says Ikkyu.

Ponder that

49

Ikkyu is wearing one of those over the top country and western jackets

Like Dolly Parton and Glen Campbell

Brilliant white, spangled with studs.

He yodels like a coyote

And with tears in his eyes

Sings *Stand by your man*

In Zen Japanese style,

Accompanied by a Shakuhachi flute

50

Ikkyu died half a millennium ago

His poems died with him.

But words seeped from his grave

Into books galore

Don't talk crap, he'd say.

Enjoy sex and keep the Buddha happy

With occasional bows.

That'll do lads and lasses

That'll do just nicely in Samsara.

Nirvana?

Whole new ball game.

END

Printed in Great Britain
by Amazon